S0-BMV-362

Jefferson Madison
Regional Library
Charlottesville, Virginia

BE A
DOCUMENT
DETECTIVE

Be a Diary Detective

March 10, 1831

Thursday Morning I went down to the bottom of the meadow to nail up the gap in the board fence. After dinner I went to the bush to see if all was right there. The weather this day was fine and warm. I was making a shoe horn today.

Kylie
Burns

Crabtree Publishing Company
www.crabtreebooks.com

30904 1661
C

BE A
DOCUMENT DETECTIVE

Author: Kylie Burns

Series research and development: Reagan Miller

Editorial director: Kathy Middleton

Editors: Janine Deschenes, Reagan Miller

Proofreader: Petrice Custance

Design: Margaret Amy Salter

Photo research: Abigail Smith

Production coordinator and prepress technician:
  Abigail Smith

Print coordinator: Margaret Amy Salter

Photographs:

iStock: annedehaas, p8

Shutterstock: © Elena Ray, p 6

Wikimedia Commons: Creative Commons, p 11

All other images from Shutterstock

Library and Archives Canada Cataloguing in Publication

Burns, Kylie, author
    Be a diary detective / Kylie Burns.

(Be a document detective)
Includes index.
Issued in print and electronic formats.
ISBN 978-0-7787-3053-8 (hardcover).--
ISBN 978-0-7787-3081-1 (softcover).--ISBN 978-1-4271-1871-4 (HTML)

    1. History--Research--Juvenile literature. 2. History--Sources--Juvenile
literature. 3. History--Methodology--Juvenile literature. 4. Biographical
sources--Juvenile literature. 5. Diaries--Juvenile literature. 6. Letters--
Juvenile literature. I. Title.

D16.B965 2017   j907.2   C2016-907107-3
                                                     C2016-907108-1

Library of Congress Cataloging-in-Publication Data

Names: Burns, Kylie, author.
Title: Be a diary detective / Kylie Burns.
Description: New York, New York : Crabtree Publishing Company, 2017. |
  Series: Be a document detective | Includes index. |
    Identifiers: LCCN 2017009737 (print) | LCCN 2017021012 (ebook) |
    ISBN 9781427118714 (Electronic HTML) |
    ISBN 9780778730538 (reinforced library binding : alk. paper) |
    ISBN 9780778730811 (pbk. : alk. paper)
Subjects: LCSH: Historiography--Juvenile literature. | History--Sources--
  Juvenile literature. | History--Research--Juvenile literature. |
  Diaries--Juvenile literature.
Classification: LCC D16 (ebook) | LCC D16 .B965 2017 (print) |
  DDC 907.2--dc23
LC record available at https://lccn.loc.gov/2017009737

Crabtree Publishing Company

www.crabtreebooks.com   1-800-387-7650

Printed in Canada/062017/MA20170420

Copyright © **2017 CRABTREE PUBLISHING COMPANY**. All rights reserved. No part of this publication may be reproduced, stored in a retrieval system or be transmitted in any form or by any means, electronic, mechanical, photocopying, recording, or otherwise, without the prior written permission of Crabtree Publishing Company. In Canada: We acknowledge the financial support of the Government of Canada through the Canada Book Fund for our publishing activities.

Published in Canada
Crabtree Publishing
616 Welland Ave.
St. Catharines, Ontario
L2M 5V6

Published in the United States
Crabtree Publishing
PMB 59051
350 Fifth Avenue, 59th Floor
New York, New York 10118

Published in the United Kingdom
Crabtree Publishing
Maritime House
Basin Road North, Hove
BN41 1WR

Published in Australia
Crabtree Publishing
3 Charles Street
Coburg North
VIC 3058

Contents

A Record of Time

Do you wonder what life was like long ago? If you could travel back in time, what questions would you ask the people you meet? Asking these kinds of questions is part of learning about **history**. History is the study of things that happened in the past. It tells us how people and places have changed over time.

History tells the story of people, places, and events from the past.

History Detectives

Historians are people who study history. They ask questions about people, places, and events from the past. Like detectives, historians look for clues to help answer their questions. Their answers can help solve mysteries about the past. Historians look for answers to questions such as:

- **How did people in the past share important news and ideas?**
- **What was daily life like for children growing up long ago?**
- **How and why do communities change?**

Daily life includes common things people do, such as going to school or doing chores around the house.

What are Primary Sources?

What do a photograph, a diary, and a map have in common? They are all examples of primary sources! Primary sources are records created by people during a certain time in history. They give **eyewitness** information about people, places, and events.

This photograph from 1937 is a primary source that shows us a kind of car that people drove during that time.

A diary is a primary source that tells about a specific time in a person's life.

Gathering Evidence

Historians study photographs, diaries, maps, and other primary sources to look for clues about the past. They use what they learn as **evidence** to support their answers to questions about the past.

This is a map of the New England region in the United States. It was drawn in the 1600s. This map is a primary source that shows the towns and cities from that time.

How are Diaries Helpful?

Primary sources include objects, photographs, and written records. Some written records, such as diaries and letters, can give a **first-hand account** of what life was like in a certain place and during a certain time. They are written by an individual in his or her own words. They help us see what life was like through someone else's eyes.

Diaries and letters often include a writer's thoughts, feelings, and descriptions of people, places, and events.

Learning from Diaries

People use diaries to record details about their daily lives. The information included in a diary depends on the person who wrote it. For example, a child might write about school, playing with friends, and doing chores around the house. An adult's diary might include details about work, family life, and community events.

January 1, 1893	Snowed pretty hard. Went and read to West a while. Lizzie is 8. Had shivered beef for breakfast & cranberry short cakes for dinner. Skated a lot yesterday on the river with [Cousins] George, Roy, Stella, and Lizzie.
January 4	16 below zero. Cold. Slid a lot this noon. West went outdoors a lot today. Had a written exercise in arithmetic and grammar ...

Detective Duty!

What details about daily life does Laura describe in her diary?

What do you learn about Laura from what you have read? What questions do you have?

The words above are from the diary of a 10-year-old girl from South Royalton, Vermont. Her name is Laura Allis Freeman. She began keeping this diary on January 1, 1893.

Point of View

Diaries give one person's **point of view** about an event or experience. Point of view is how a person sees things. A person's point of view can depend on their age, where they live, and their background. People with different points of view may describe the same event differently. Historians read different people's diaries and study other primary sources to get more information to answer questions about life in the past.

Some of the earliest diaries were painted on cave walls using pictures and symbols to tell stories about daily life. These pictures above show how people hunted animals for food long ago.

Keeping Diaries

Most diaries in the past were written on paper. Over time, paper breaks down and turns yellow. Many diaries are kept in museums to keep them from being lost or damaged. People can then read and learn from these primary sources for many years.

These diaries belong to a famous inventor named Charles Babbage. His diaries include some of his ideas for inventions and the steps he took to create them. His diaries are kept in the Science Museum in London, England.

Detective Duty!

Why do you think it is important to keep diaries in museums? What do you think you could learn by reading Charles Babbage's diaries?

Questions
and Answers

A diary can help us understand more about what life was like for the person who wrote it. Studying diaries helps us make connections between ourselves and others who lived long ago. Diaries usually include the date each **entry** was written, so they are very useful records for learning about specific times or events.

Historians ask questions when they read diaries and search the entries for answers. Some questions may not be answered, but every piece of information helps. Some questions document detectives may ask include:

- Who wrote the diary? When did they write it?
- What was important in the daily lives of people at that time in history?
- How are things different today than in the past?
- What facts can we learn from the diary to better understand a certain time, place, or event?

A Farmgirl's Diary

The diary entry below was written by Louisa Collins, a girl who lived on a farm in Nova Scotia, Canada in the 1800s.

September 1, 1815
This has been a very rainy day, and I have been sewing all day till about five o'clock when it left off raining and Mama and me went and picked some peas and beans [...] It is so cold this evening that I have been sitting by the fire. Winter approaches very fast and we have had very little warm weather.

Louisa Collins, a girl living on a farm in Nova Scotia, wrote this diary entry on September 1, 1815.

It was important to get food from the farm and finish chores such as sewing.

Louisa kept warm near a fire. My family has a heated home to keep warm.

We have learned that it was often cold and rainy that year in Nova Scotia. We know that children who lived on farms during the 1800s did a lot of work.

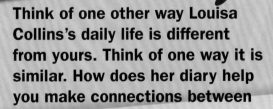

Detective Duty!

Think of one other way Louisa Collins's daily life is different from yours. Think of one way it is similar. How does her diary help you make connections between her life and yours?

Diary of a Settler

Diaries can give us eyewitness information about important time periods in history. Settlers are people who arrive to live in a new place where few or no others live. Settlers created some of the first towns and cities. William Helliwell was a settler who lived in **Upper Canada**. He wrote diaries that give an eyewitness account of the lives of settlers there.

March 10, 1831
Thursday Morning I went down to the bottom of the meadow to nail up the gap in the board fence. After dinner I went to the bush to see if all was right there. The weather this day was fine and warm. I was making a shoe horn today.

William Helliwell, a settler in Upper Canada, wrote this diary entry on March 10, 1831.

It seems important for William to fix the fence that protects his house. Maybe settlers were worried wild animals would come in.

We have learned that it was warm in Upper Canada in March that year. William lived near a meadow, where grass and other plants grow.

We need to learn more, such as what a shoehorn is. Do people still use those today?

More Questions

William Helliwell's diary can help us answer questions about the weather and landscape in Upper Canada, and the types of jobs that settlers had to do there. But it's normal to have questions that can't be answered when looking at primary sources. Look for more information by checking online, asking a historian at a museum, or visiting the library.

Detective Duty!

- **Use evidence from William Helliwell's diary to describe what the land was like in Upper Canada in 1831.**
- **What questions do you still have after reading his diary? Where could you find answers?**

Learning about Letters

Letters are also first-hand accounts of a person's experiences, feelings, and daily life. Letters have dates and are addressed, or sent to, someone else. When people write letters, they describe their thoughts and feelings to another person. We can read letters to learn about life during certain times and in certain places. This letter was written to the United States First Lady Eleanor Roosevelt by a young girl during the **Great Depression**, a time in history when many people were very poor.

Gravette, Arkansas
Nov. 6, 1936

Dear Mrs. Roosevelt,
I am writing to you for some of your old soiled dresses if you have any. [...] I am in the seventh grade but I have to stay out of school because I have no books or clothes to wear. I am in need of dresses & slips and a coat very bad. [...]

Yours Truly,
Miss L.H

A girl living in Arkansas wrote this letter on November 6, 1936.

We have learned that some people at this time did not have things they need, such as clothing.

It seems important to the girl to get the clothing she needs and to go back to school. Daily life was very different for people then. This letter shows that people were worried about not having the things they need.

This girl cannot go to school. I am able to go to school every day.

Read All About It!

Other kinds of written records can also offer information about the past. Newspaper articles sometimes include **quotes** from primary sources and eyewitnesses about certain times and places. Speeches and even food recipes can also teach us about the daily lives of people who lived in the past.

Many children, just like the child who wrote to Mrs. Roosevelt, write letters and diaries that describe their daily lives and experiences. You can, too!

Detective Duty!

- Have you ever received a letter from someone?
- What information is included in a letter?
- How is a letter like a diary?
- How is it different?

Changing Times

Change happens when people develop new ways of doing things and new tools to use. We call these tools **technology**. Technology changes and improves over time to create better, faster ways of doing work. Improvements in technology over time have changed the way people keep diaries and send letters.

Vlogging, or video blogging, is a popular way to keep a diary today. Vloggers record videos to share their thoughts and feelings with others.

Computer Technology

A computer is a type of technology that helps people do work. Today, many people use computers to write and **preserve** their thoughts, feelings, and experiences. Video diaries and **blogs** are two of the tools people use to record their thoughts and experiences online. They are modern ways of keeping track of specific times or events.

Emails are a way that people send and receive letters online.

Detective Duty!

- **Can you think of other ways technology helps us keep track of our lives today?**
- **Why is it useful to be able to read diaries and letters online?**

Framing our Past

If you took pictures of family and friends, what would you do with them? You would probably display them in a photo album or picture frame to remind you of people and events in your life. A diary does the same thing with our stories. Sometimes, people include pictures and sketches to go along with diary entries or letters. These help someone remember a person, object, place, or event. We can learn a lot from the words and images people include in diaries and letters.

People often add photographs to travel diaries to record exactly what a place, object, or event looked like. This helps them remember an awesome vacation for years to come!

Write It!

Diaries can tell about a person's daily life. They can also describe important events and fun traditions. Choose an event, holiday, or tradition that your family has celebrated and write a diary entry about it. Include details such as the date and place, who was there, what you did, and why it was special to you. What do you think future document detectives will be able to learn about your life by reading your diary entry?

You could write about your brother's birthday party, last Friday's family movie night, or a fun family vacation you took together. The possibilities are endless!

Think about it

Challenge

Why not take it a step further and start your own daily diary? Try writing something every day for one month. You can write about your daily life, such as the things you learned at school, the chores you did at home, or important events or activities. At the end of the month, read your diary from beginning to end. Did it help you remember details about a time or event? If you enjoyed this challenge, keep up the habit of writing your thoughts every day!

Do you remember all of the different ways you can keep a diary? You can write on paper, record a vlog, or type a blog. Which type of diary will you choose to make?

Learning More

There are many places you can visit to find out more about primary sources. Start with your local museum and library. Churches, community groups, and schools are also good places to find information.

These books and websites will help you learn more:

Books

Bruno Clapper, Nikki. *Learning about Primary Sources.* Capstone Press, 2015.

Kalman, Bobbie. *Communication: Then and Now*. Crabtree Publishing, 2014.

Mays, Osceola, and Govenar, Alan B. *Osceola: Memories of a Sharecropper's Daughter*. Hyperion Books for Children, 2000.

Websites

www.brookhousepress.ca/louisa/textltd.htm
Read all the entries of Louisa Collins's diary at this website.

http://vermonthistory.org/educate/online-resources/history-journals-in-class/part-1-historical-journals
Visit this link to access the diaries of Laura Freeman and Porter Perrin, two young people who grew up in Virginia during in the 1800s. The diaries describe daily life including school, chores, and transportation.

www.history.org/kids/
Check out this site from the Colonial Williamsburg Foundation. It contains cool facts, interactive activities, and even has an online tour of the historic town of Colonial Williamsburg.

www.girlonawhaleship.org/jernapp/laura.do
This website has stories, information, and interactive activities based on the diary of Laura Jernegan, a young girl who lived and traveled with her family on a whaling ship in the Pacific Ocean from 1868-1871.

Words to Know

blogs   A website regularly updated with a person's thoughts; an online diary

emails   Messages or letters sent and received online

entry   An individual item written in a diary or as part of a list

evidence   Information that can help prove something else is either true or false

eyewitness   A person who sees something happen and can tell us about it

first-hand account   A story or source, such as a diary, that came directly from someone who experienced or witnessed an event

Great Depression   A period of time, from 1929 to 1939, when many people around the world did not have jobs and were very poor

history   The study of past events

historian   A person who studies past events

point of view   How a person sees things based on their beliefs and experiences

preserve   To keep something how it originally was

quotes   Parts of a person's speech that are repeated later, often in the news

technology   The tools people use to do work, which change and improve over time

Upper Canada   The name for an area of land in today's Ontario, Canada that was ruled by Great Brit and existed from 1791 to 1841

vlogging   To record one's thoughts on video to keep for oneself or share online

Index

About the Author:

Kylie Burns is a writer and teacher. She has written several children's books on a wide rang of interesting topics. She loves researching primary sources. Once, she even discovered some of her ancestors' personal artifacts, letters, and photos on display in a museum.

MAR 2010
WITHDRAWN